Practise Writing

Practise Writing

Mary Stephens

Eurocentre Bournemouth

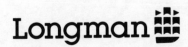 

Longman Group UK Limited
Longman House, Burnt Mill, Harlow,
Essex CM20 2JE, England
and Associated Companies throughout the world.

First published 1986
Fifteenth impression 1993

ISBN 0-582-79107-3

Illustrated by Pat Tourret (B.L. Kearley Ltd); Jerry
Collins, David Etchell and John Ridyard.

Set in 10/12 Times, Linotron 202

Printed in Malaysia by CL

Acknowledgements

We are grateful to the following for permission to
reproduce copyright photographs:

Brenard Press Ltd for page 27 (left); Camera Press
Ltd for pages 9, 23 & 57 (bottom); J. Allan Cash
Photolibrary for page 42; International Photobank for
page 14; London Features International Ltd for page
31 (top left) & 31 (bottom left); Longman
Photographic Unit for page 72; Picturepoint-London
for pages 57 (top) & 77: Syndication International Ltd
for page 26; Copyright © by Universal Pictures, a
Division of Universal City Studios, Inc. Courtesy of
MCA Publishing Rights, a Division of MCA Inc.
National Film Archive, London for page 60.

The interview with Paul McCartney of page 31 is
fictitious.

Introduction

Practise Writing is designed for students at the intermediate level of language learning. Many books which now stress the importance of oral communication skills tend to neglect the written side of the language, especially as regards extensive written tasks.

This course is intended to fill the gap, by providing thorough practice in a wide variety of different types of written English, including extensive coverage of the main types of written task which the student is required to study for the Cambridge First Certificate in English Composition Paper. The techniques, structures and vocabulary which are needed to produce written material such as letters, narratives, descriptions, speeches, dialogues and opinions are all examined in detail using clear models and guided practice.

A writing lesson can often become a rather tedious 'book-bound' activity, but *Practise Writing* has been devised to include a number of communicative activities, such as pair practice, discussion and simple roleplay, so that a lesson can easily be phased to hold the student's attention and interest.

Each unit of *Practise Writing* contains a model composition of some 200 words. The Notes which follow provide a brief analysis of the model with regard to such areas as paragraph planning, register and style. The student is then provided with practice in some of the areas of grammar, vocabulary and sentence-linking which are the basic requirements for the particular task in hand. The concluding section of each unit — Written tasks — gives the student the opportunity to write full-length compositions, utilising the structures and skills which have previously been practised.

Contents

Contents

Writing a dialogue

Susan Kelly is a journalist. She works for one of the big daily newspapers in Fleet Street and her work often takes her abroad.

1

Susan's passport runs out this year, so she is applying for a new one. Study the information she gives on her application form, then use the following prompts to ask questions about her:

Where/she/born?   What/surname?
Married?   What/Christian names?
What/date/birth?   What/address/telephone number?
Which town/born in?   Which country/live in?
How old?   What/job?

Name __Susan Kelly__
Occupation __Journalist__
Signature __Sue Kelly__

Please write in CAPITAL LETTERS and in ink

1 TO BE FILLED IN BY ALL APPLICANTS

	Mr	Mrs	Miss	Ms	or title
Tick correct box	☐	☐	✓	☐	_____

Your surname __KELLY__

Christian names or forenames __SUSAN CLARE__

Maiden surname (if applicable) __✓__

	Married	Single	Widowed	Divorced	Separated
Tick correct box	☐	✓	☐	☐	☐

Age last birthday __23__ Country of birth __ENGLAND__

Present address __17 ENFIELD COURT, ENFIELD ROAD, TWICKENHAM, MIDDLESEX__ Postcode __MY6 3PQ__

Daytime telephone no __894-0556__
(We may need to get in touch with you urgently)

Job/occupation __JOURNALIST__

Town of birth __LEICESTER__

Date of birth __5-8-1961__

Country of residence __ENGLAND__

2

Now find out similar information about your partner. Write down the questions you will need to ask in full, then interview your partner and note down his/her answers. Don't forget to ask for the spelling of names or towns when necessary!

Dialogue

Look at the dialogue below. Read it aloud with your partner. Susan is just leaving the post office when she bumps into an old friend.

VOCABULARY

good heavens
an expression of surprise

bump into
meet by chance

What are you up to?
(very informal)
What are you doing?

actually
in fact

I'm finding my feet.
I'm getting used to my new job.

I'd better dash now.
I'd better hurry.

cheerio
goodbye

Dave: Good heavens! It's Sue, isn't it? Do you remember me? We were at school together.

Sue: Dave! I don't believe it! How are you?

Dave: Fine! What about you? What are you up to these days? Do you work near here?

Sue: Yes, I'm a journalist, actually. I work just round the corner, in Fleet Street.

Dave: A journalist, eh? That must be an interesting job! How long have you been doing that?

Sue: Oh, not very long — I'm still finding my feet really. But what about you? Are you still single or did you and Pat get married in the end?

Dave: Oh, we got married last year. We live in Birmingham now. Look, why don't you come up and visit us sometime? Pat would love to see you again.

Sue: Oh yes, that's a lovely idea. Er. . . I know, give me your number and I'll give you a ring this week sometime. We can arrange things then, can't we?

Dave: OK, fine! It's 84–698–0226. I'll look forward to that.

Sue: Me too! Well, I'd better dash now or I'll be late.

Dave: Oh, right then. Don't forget to ring!

Sue: I won't! Cheerio for now.

Notes

A A good, written dialogue should read as realistic, lively conversation. You can make your dialogues sound natural by including:

GAP-FILLING WORDS: Oh. . . Er. . . Well. . . Let's see. . .
OK. . . Fine. . . Look. . .
By the way. . . Anyway. . .

QUESTION TAGS: . . ., isn't it?
. . ., can't you?
. . ., doesn't it?

APPROPRIATE FUNCTIONAL LANGUAGE

Look at these examples of functional language:

STARTING A CONVERSATION	Goodness, it's hot/cold in here, isn't it? Good heavens! It's (X), isn't it? Fancy bumping into you!
SHOWING SURPRISE	Gosh! Good heavens! Goodness! Good Lord!
ARRANGING A MEETING	Perhaps we could meet again sometime. What about getting together sometime?
MAKING SUGGESTIONS	How about . . .ing? Do you fancy . . .ing?
SAYING GOODBYE	Look forward to seeing you next week, then. Well, it was lovely to see you again! Well, I must dash! Take care, now.

B   Always consider carefully the situation and the people involved in the dialogue before you choose your style. In the model dialogue, Susan is speaking to an old friend, so the language is friendly and informal. She would probably *not* use such informal language when speaking to her boss, otherwise she might sound impolite. Look at these examples:

INFORMAL	FORMAL
What are you up to?	What are you doing?
Cheerio.	Goodbye.
Right then.	Yes, all right.

An informal dialogue

Imagine you have just met an old friend. Provide the missing part of the conversation. Be as natural as possible.

A: Good gracious! It's (X), isn't it? Do you remember me? We were at school together.

B: . . . . . .

A: Oh, I'm fine! And you? What are you up to these days?

B: . . . . . .

A: Really? How long have you been doing that?

B: . . . . . .

A: Me? Oh, I'm a nurse — I'm on my way to the hospital now, actually. Look, do you live near here? Perhaps we could meet for a chat sometime.

B: . . . . . .

A: Mm, that's a good idea! I love Italian food. Look, give me your phone number and I'll give you a ring later this week.

B: . . . . . .

A: Me, too! Bye for now then!

A formal dialogue

Here is a more formal conversation between doctor and patient. Complete the doctor's part of the conversation.

Doctor: Hello. Come in and sit down.
Patient: Hello, Dr Jones.
Doctor: . . . . . . ?
Patient: Well, I think I've sprained my wrist.
Doctor: . . . . . . ?
Patient: Yesterday morning. I was playing tennis, you see, and I tripped and fell over.
Doctor: . . . . . . ?
Patient: Well, it didn't seem so bad yesterday, so I thought it would be all right. But this morning it's very swollen and I just can't use it.
Doctor: . . . . . . ?
Patient: Ouch, yes! That hurts a lot!
Doctor: . . . .
Patient: Yes, I see. Thank you very much, Dr Jones. Goodbye.

Roleplay

You are on a plane flying home from your holidays. You get into conversation with a passenger sitting beside you. Each of you should:

— find some excuse to start talking.
— ask the other person about himself (his job/his family/his hobbies etc).
— tell him about yourself.
— arrange to meet again.
— decide where and when to meet.
— bring the conversation to a logical conclusion.

Written tasks

1 Write down the conversation which took place in the roleplay exercise above. Give the name of each speaker, followed by the words spoken.

Example: *Passenger:* Excuse me, have you got the right time?
Student: Yes, of course. It's 8.05 exactly.
By the way, . . .

2 You borrowed your father's car this evening to go to a party. Unfortunately, you damaged it. With a partner, work out the conversation which took place between you and your father when you got home. Be as dramatic as possible! Tell him what happened and why, and how you are going to repay him. Then write out the conversation in dialogue form. Use the language in the box to help you.

	USEFUL LANGUAGE
APOLOGISING	I'm afraid I've got some bad news for you . . . I'm afraid I've damaged/ruined/broken . . . I'm terribly/awfully/really sorry. I know I should/shouldn't have . . .
SHOWING SURPRISE AND ANGER	Oh no, what have you done to it? You haven't . . . . . . , have you? Honestly, (X), how could you be so careless!
EXPLAINING WHAT HAPPENED	I was just . . . . . . when . . . It happened while I was . . .
OFFERING COMPENSATION	Look, don't worry. I'll buy you a new one/pay for the damage.

UNIT 2

A letter to a friend

Susan's boyfriend is on a working holiday in Ireland. This is the letter she has just received from him.

16 O'Donnell St,
Castlebar,
County Mayo,
EIRE
16th June 1986

Dear Sue,

Now that I've been here for a few days, I thought I had better write and let you know how I'm getting on in this beautiful country.

When I first arrived, I couldn't get used to the slow pace of life! However, I'm gradually learning to take things easy, and I'm beginning to feel really at home. My first impression of the Irish is that they are really friendly and helpful people - and they certainly know how to enjoy life!

I'm staying at a little guest house here in Castlebar. The countryside round about is marvellous, and I've been doing a lot of walking and fishing. I've made friends with some of the people in the village, and we spend most evenings in the local pub chatting - and drinking Guinness, of course!

Well, I must rush now to catch the post. Do drop me a line when you have time. I miss you!

Love,
Tom

Notes

A

Study Tom's letter and then answer the following questions:

1 Where do you put your address and the date when you write an informal letter?
2 Should you write your name at the top of the letter?
3 Where should you write the salutation (*Dear Sue* etc)?
4 Where should you begin the first paragraph of your letter?

B

A letter usually contains the following stages:

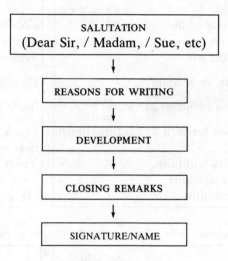

You should use at least one paragraph for each of the main stages.

C

Notice that Tom's letter is a friendly letter, so the vocabulary and structures are informal. Some examples of informal and formal styles are given below. Always think about who you are writing to before you begin your letter. Mistakes in style make your letter look odd or impolite.

INFORMAL	FORMAL
I've been here . . .	I have been here . . .
I thought I'd better just write and let you know that . . .	I am writing to inform you that . . .
Well, I must rush now to catch the post. Do drop me a line . . .	I look forward to hearing from you in the near future.
Love, . . .	Yours faithfully,/ Yours sincerely, . . .

D Notice that formal and informal letters are laid out differently.

FORMAL

```
                              your address
address of the        date
person you are
writing to

Dear Sir/Madam,

(main points of the letter)

I look forward to hearing from
you.
Yours faithfully,
your signature
(M. Smith)
```

FORMAL

```
                              your address
address of the        date
person you are
writing to

Dear Mr Smith,

(main points of the letter)

I look forward to meeting you
next week.
Yours sincerely,
your signature
(D. Jones)
```

INFORMAL

```
                         your address
                         date
Dear Mrs Jackson,

    (main points of the letter)

    Looking forward to seeing
you.
    Best wishes/Yours/Regards,
    your signature/name
```

VERY FRIENDLY

```
                              your address
                              date
Dear John,

    (main points of the letter)

    Do write back soon.
    Love/Best wishes,
      your name
```

Spot the mistakes

The letter below contains several serious errors. Work with a partner to write the letter out again correctly.

```
        Dave Smith
        charles street, 66
        bristol
        october 9th, 1986

    Hello Anne!
Just a quick line to say that I'll be in London on
Wednesday and to ask if you'd like to meet me for
lunch. I'm sorry this is such short notice, but I
only heard about the meeting yesterday. I really do
hope you can come as I've got a lot of news to give
you and I'd like your advice on a couple of things.
Anyway, let me know as soon as possible - maybe you
could give me a ring tonight? Well, I must dash now.
Hope to hear from you soon
yours faithfully, Dave
```

Recent activities

> I've made friends with some of the people.
> I've been doing a lot of fishing.

Remember that we often use the Present Perfect tenses for actions which took place at an unspecified time in the past. They are also used when the action or the time is not yet finished. Use the prompts below to write questions and then interview your partner.

How long / you / learn / English?
How much / you / learn / this year?
You / do / lot / homework / since / beginning / term?
What / you / do / your spare time / recently?
You / go / theatre / this month?
You / work / hard / today?

Vocabulary practice

Form adjectives from the following nouns.

Example: happiness — *happy*

friend	kindness	rudeness
help	patience	sympathy
industry	reserve	talk

Giving advice

> I thought I had better write.

1   Imagine your partner has got a number of problems. Give him/her some advice, using the construction shown above.

Example: He/She has a headache.
You say: *I think you'd/you had better take an aspirin.*

Imagine he/she:

— feels sick.
— is homesick.
— is having difficulty making friends.
— hasn't done the homework.
— can't stop smoking.

2   Now get your partner to tell you some of his/her problems (real or imaginary). Offer some practical advice.

Discussion

Talk about the problems of visiting, or living in, a foreign country.

If you are living abroad now:

How are you getting on so far? Are you homesick?
What do you miss?
Can you remember how you felt when you first arrived?
What has been the most difficult thing for you to get used to doing?
What have you been doing lately, both at school and at home?
What are/were your first impressions of this country?

If you are still in your own country:

When did you last spend some time abroad? Where?
What were your first impressions of the country? Did these change?
Can you remember how you felt when you first arrived?
What was the most difficult thing for you to get used to?
How did you spend your time in the day/evening?

Written tasks

1 Use the prompts given below to write a complete letter:

> King's Hotel,
> Buckingham Avenue,
> London W1
>
> 20th June 1986
>
> Dear Pablo,
>   Now / we / be / here / one / week / I / think / I / better / write / tell / you / how / we / get / on.
>   When / we / first / arrive / we / can / not / understand / anyone ! However / we / be / slowly / get / use / to / everything / and / begin / enjoy / ourselves. English people / be / very helpful / and / friendly / but / they / be / always / in a hurry !
>   We / stay / hotel / near Oxford Street. Of course / we / already / do / a lot / sightseeing / and also go / theatre / every night. I / do / plenty / shopping / too. Some things / be / really / quite cheap!
>   Well / must / dash / now / post / letter. We / really / look / forward / see / you / when / we / get back / next month.
>   Love,
>   *Maria*

USEFUL LANGUAGE

I wondered if you'd
   like to . . .
How about . . . ?
We could . . .
I think you'd
   enjoy . . .
Let me know if . . .

---

2 You are spending a few weeks abroad. Write a brief letter to a friend, telling him/her about your recent activities.

3 In pairs, decide how you would like to spend this weekend. Then write a letter to a mutual friend, inviting him/her to spend the weekend with you and suggesting how you could spend the time together. Use the language in the box on the left to help you.

A formal letter

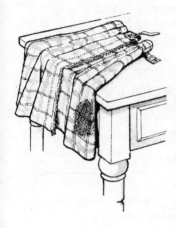

This summer, Susan spent her holidays in Scotland.
She bought a kilt, but when she got home she
discovered it was flawed. This is the letter which
she wrote to the shop to complain about it.

Notes

A

Look at Susan's letter
and then answer the
following questions:

1 Where do you put your
address when you write
a formal letter?
2 Where do you put your
name?
3 Where do you put
the number of
your house/flat in
an address?
4 Where do you put the
date?

Remember that in a
formal letter the address
of the person you are
writing to is usually
included.

---

17 Enfield Court,
Enfield Road,
Twickenham,
Middlesex MY6 3PQ

Ross Wool Mills,   5th July 1986
Glenross,
Edinburgh

Dear Sir,

I am writing to you about a tartan kilt which
I bought from your shop while on holiday this
summer.

When I took it out of the bag and examined it
closely, I found a large, black mark at the
side. As you will realise, I was extremely
upset to discover this flaw. At your prices,
I expect top quality!

I am returning the kilt with this letter and
look forward to receiving a full refund of
£40.50.

Yours faithfully,

Sue Kelly

Susan Kelly

19

B

The first paragraph of a formal letter usually states the reason for writing. Some useful phrases are:

> Thank you for your letter of . . .
> I was sorry to learn from your letter that . . .
> I saw your advertisement in the local newspaper
>   and would like to . . .
> I am writing to you about . . .
> I am writing to apologise for . . .

The middle paragraph usually contains the body of your letter and explains the situation in detail. (You may use more than one paragraph for this.)

The conclusion of your letter should normally include some polite remark such as:

> I look forward to hearing from you soon.
> Would you please let me know as soon as possible whether . . .
> Please accept my apologies for any inconvenience.
> I would be grateful if you would . . .

Salutations and endings

Study the language shown in the boxes below, then answer the questions.

1 Dear Sir/Madam,	2 Dear Mr Smith,
Yours faithfully,	Yours sincerely,

3 Dear Mrs Jones,	4 Dear John,
Best wishes, *or* Yours truly,	Love, *or* Regards, *or* Best wishes,

Which of the above would you use when writing to:

— your landlady?
— your friends?
— the manager of a company? (You do not know his/her name.)
— the Principal of your college?

Addresses and dates

Write out the following addresses and dates correctly:

smith street 269
november 16th 1984
england london

august 9th 1983
fitzgerald avenue 28
john brown ltd
oxford

Beginning a letter

> I am writing to you about a tartan kilt which I bought from your shop while on holiday this summer.

Look at the box above and then write opening sentences for letters on the following topics:

1 You weren't able to attend a meeting last week because you were ill. You want to apologise.

2 You received an expensive gift from a relative for Christmas. You want to thank him.

3 You have seen an interesting job advertisement in the newspaper. You would like to know more.

4 You have passed your examination. You want to inform your prospective employers.

5 The noise from the local disco kept you awake all night. You want to complain.

Making complaints

> When I took it out of the bag and examined it closely, I found a large, black mark at the side.

Look at the box above. What sort of complaint might you make about the following articles?

Example:

a record

You write: *The first time I played it, I found that it was scratched.*

1 a book
2 a handbag
3 a pair of shoes
4 a game
5 a sweater

21

A scrambled letter

The sentences in the letter on the right are in the wrong order. Unscramble them and then write the letter again, setting out the facts in logical paragraphs.

159 Saxby Road,
Leicester,
LC9 3PQ

16th November 1986

Marks & Spencer,
Oxford Street,
London W1

Dear Sir,

I would be grateful if you would let me know whether anybody has handed it in and if it would be possible to have it sent to me.

It is a gentleman's gold digital watch with a black strap and with the initials J.E. inscribed on the back.

I am writing to enquire about a gold watch which I think I lost in your store last Saturday morning.

I look forward to hearing from you.

Although it is not very valuable, it is of great sentimental value. I will, of course, send on the cost of postage if necessary.

Yours faithfully,

John Edwards

John Edwards

Describing objects

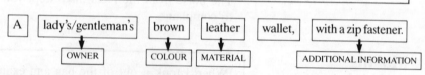

A	lady's/gentleman's	brown	leather	wallet,	with a zip fastener.
	OWNER	COLOUR	MATERIAL		ADDITIONAL INFORMATION

Notice the usual order of adjectives, shown above, then describe the articles illustrated below. Use your imagination to describe colours Use the language in the box on the left to help you.

USEFUL LANGUAGE
lady's/gentleman's/child's/boy's/girl's
leather/plastic/cotton/woollen/glass
gold/silver
with a strap/a pop fastener/a zip fastener
with long/short handles
with the initials/name/(X) inscribed/written/printed on it

Written tasks

1 You have been sent a gift for Christmas but there is something wrong with it. Write to the shop/manufacturer's to complain. Set your letter out clearly, with the address included, as in the model at the beginning of this unit.

2 While staying at a hotel some distance from your home, you lost something valuable. Write a letter to the hotel manager, describing what you lost and where you might have left it. Set your letter out clearly, with the address included, as in the model letter at the beginning of this unit.

Writing a biography

Which world figure do you most admire? Why?
Should more be done to help the developing countries?
In what form should this help be given?

Last week, Susan was sent to India to write an article on 1979 Nobel
Peace Prize winner, Mother Teresa.

Notes

A
When doing any written
work, it is important to
plan what you are going
to write before you
begin.

B
A biography must be
arranged so that events
follow on in a logical
order. In the article,
each big change in
Mother Teresa's life has
been covered in a
separate paragraph.

C
Always bring your
composition to a logical
conclusion. A story
which stops in mid-air is
disappointing to the
reader.

D
Read the biography
again and answer the
following questions:

1 Which periods of
Mother Teresa's life are
covered in the first three
paragraphs?

2 Which verb tenses are
used in these paragraphs?

3 In the final paragraph
we read a little about her
life now. Which tenses
are used here?

MOTHER TERESA

Mother Teresa was born in Skopje, Yugoslavia, on August 27th 1910. She grew up with her brother and sister in a very happy family, and attended the government school near her home until she was eighteen. At that time, some missionaries from Yugoslavia were working in Calcutta, and they often wrote to the school about their work. She decided to join them.

When she finished school, she went first to Ireland and after that to India, where she began to train for the religious life. After training, she was sent to Calcutta, where she taught Geography at a high school and eventually became Principal.

However, although she loved teaching, in 1946 Mother Teresa left the school and went to work in the slums of Calcutta. She did some nursing training in Patna, and then began her work helping the poor and comforting the dying in the streets of the city. Gradually, others came to help her, and her work spread to other parts of India.

Mother Teresa is now a well-known figure. Dressed in her white and blue sari, she has been photographed all over the world, as she travels to open new schools and hospitals in poor countries. In 1979, she was awarded the Nobel Peace Prize — a small tribute to the lifetime of love and service she has given to the poor.

Word search

Find words in the text which correspond to the following:

went to school   slowly/little by little
people sent out to teach their   famous
    religion   she was given (as a prize)
to learn how to do a job   something given to someone to
streets of small, dirty,   show admiration or respect
    crowded houses
in the end

Word order

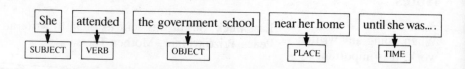

Study the language shown above, then rearrange the following sentences:

1 she / to school / for six years / went
2 at college / they / Computer Studies / for five years / took
3 since 1978 / in Zurich / I have been working
4 to go / to South America / hope / next year / I
5 for six years / in Spain / I / worked

Training or apprenticeship?

> I trained as a secretary.
> I did an apprenticeship in engineering.

Notice that, in general, people in manual jobs do an *apprenticeship*; people in the clerical or professional fields *train* for their jobs.

1 Would the following people train or do an apprenticeship?

    a bank clerk   a gardener   a teacher
    a car mechanic   a nurse

2 Did you train or do an apprenticeship? Write a sentence about yourself as in the model above.

Discussion

Use the following prompts to write questions and then interview your partner about his/her life. Make a note of the answers. You will need the information later.

Where / you / born?
How many people / be / there / your family?
What / your father / mother / do?

Where / you / grow up?
What / it / like?
How long / you / attend / secondary school?
What / your school / like?

What / you / do / after / leave / school?
Apprenticeship or training?
What / be / your first job? Where?

You / change / your job / since then?
What / you / do / now?
How long?
What / it / like?

What / you / do / spare time?
Married? Children?

What / your / ambition?
What / you / intend / do / future?

Linking information

Ben worked hard at school and got a place at a technical college. *After* getting his diploma, he joined a building firm *but* he found the work boring *and* left. *Next/Then* he got a job abroad. He got on well and *some time later*, was able to set up his own business. *Eventually* he became a millionaire.

Notice the use of linking words in the paragraph above. Write similar paragraphs, linking the sentences below. Choose from the linking words provided.

after	eventually	some time later
and	in the end	then
but	next	

PAUL'S CAREER

Paul left school at the age of 18.
He went to college.
He failed his exams.
He had to leave.
He went to work in a bank.
He worked very hard.
He was promoted to Assistant Manager.
He became the manager of the bank.

ANGELA'S CAREER

Angela gave up her job.
She set out to travel round the world.
She ran out of money.
She came home.
She began working for a newspaper.
She was very good at the job.
She got a job with the BBC.
She became the editor of a top television programme.

Written tasks

1 In 1973, Clare Francis sailed across the Atlantic singlehanded. Since then, she has become one of Britain's most well-known sportswomen. Use the prompts below to build up a complete biography:

Clare Francis / born / Surrey / April 17th, 1946. She / attend / Royal School of Ballet / and / then / win / place / University College, London / where / study / Economics.

   After / leave / university, / she / begin / career / marketing / but / she / soon / become / bored / city life. She / love / sailing, / and / when / uncle / die / and / leave / her / money, / she / decide / buy / own boat. Then, / 1973, / she / set out / sail / across / Atlantic / America, / singlehanded.

   Since then, Clare Francis / become / popular figure / radio / television. She / take part / many singlehanded races / and / write / and / present / television series / ships / sailing. 1977 / she / marry / Frenchman, / Jaques Redon, and they / have / one son.

   In / free time / she / enjoy / read, / garden, / and music, / and / she / recently / publish / first novel, / 'Night Sky'. She / now / live / Lymington, / popular yachting resort / South coast / England.

2 Use the information you collected in the Discussion exercise to write about your partner's life.

3 Write a short biography of the person you think is one of the most outstanding figures living today.

Writing notes and messages

Susan shares a London flat with a girl called Anne, an air hostess with British Airways. This weekend, Anne is due back from a two-week flight to Kenya. As Susan will be away for the weekend, she has left Anne a message.

Notes

A

When writing notes and messages it is essential to set out the information so that it is clear. For this reason each new piece of information is usually placed on a new line.

B

You will have noticed that certain words tend to be omitted when writing notes and messages. Examples of some of these are given here:

> Anne
>
> Hope you had a good trip! Gone to Bristol for the weekend - back Monday morning.
>
> Have left plenty of food in fridge - starting diet on Monday so please eat everything!
>
> David called Thursday - will call again Sunday am.
>
> Rent due this Sat. Have left cheque in bedroom under vase.
>
> Please feed cat! Tin in cupboard under sink.
>
> See you Mon!
> Sue

	FULL FORM	NOTE FORM
PRONOUNS	*I* hope you had . . .	Hope you had . . .
ARTICLES	I hope you had *a* good trip.	Hope you had good trip.
VERBS (usually the auxillaries *to be* and *to have*)	The tin *is* in the cupboard.	Tin in cupboard.
SOME PREPOSITIONS	David called *on* Thursday.	David called Thursday.
POSSESSIVE PRONOUNS	I'm starting *my* diet . . .	Starting diet . . .

Vocabulary practice

The following abbreviations are often found in notes and messages. Say what they mean. Can you add any more to this list?

NB	PTO
eg	Mon/Tues
am/pm	etc
&	v enjoyable
ie	re

Interpreting messages

Below are some typical messages. What would you say if you were actually *speaking* to the person in question?

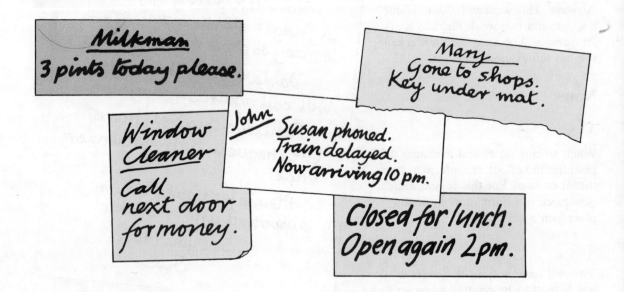

Milkman
3 pints today please.

Mary
Gone to shops.
Key under mat.

Window
Cleaner
Call
next door
for money.

John
Susan phoned.
Train delayed.
Now arriving 10 pm.

Closed for lunch.
Open again 2pm.

Writing messages

Imagine you share a flat with Susan. Write some messages for the following situations:

1 You have gone to the cinema. You have left some supper in the fridge.

2 Susan's boss, Mr Grey, phoned at 6 pm. He will call back later.

3 The television isn't working. Someone is coming to repair it sometime after 3 pm.

4 There is a party at 10, Smith Street. If Susan wants to come, she should bring a bottle.

5 You have lost your front door key. You want Susan to leave her key under the mat, if she goes out.

Making notes

Anne's boyfriend, Carlos, is looking for a new flat in London. As he has been called away on business, Anne has agreed to look round the flat for him and to make a few notes.

In pairs, read the dialogue between Anne and the landlord.

Landlord: Ah, good afternoon. You are the young lady who rang this morning, I presume?

Anne: Yes, that's right. I've come about the flat. As I told you on the phone, it's actually my boyfriend, Carlos, who is interested — but there was an emergency and he had to go back to Spain for a few days. So I promised I'd come and have a look at the flat for him.

Landlord: Fine. Well, let's start here in the living room, shall we? As you see, it's quite a large room, and it gets plenty of sunshine. The walls are nice and thick so you can't hear anything from next door.

Anne: Mmm. . . What about heating?

Landlord: Well, there's the electric fire, of course, and there's a paraffin heater in the attic if it gets really cold.

(*They go into the kitchen.*)

Anne: Gosh, it's rather small, isn't it? I mean, there's barely enough room for the two of us in here!

Landlord: Well, just a minute — it's only a single flat, remember. There's plenty of cupboard space under the sink. And there's a brand new cooker, and a fridge, look.

Anne: Yes, that's true, I suppose. Can we have a look at the bedroom now?

Landlord: Yes, just through here. You see, it's a lovely, big room — it's just been redecorated and there are plenty of cupboards and built-in wardrobes over there.

Anne: Yes, it is a nice room — but there's no heating at all in here, is there?

Landlord: Well, no, but I could let Mr Alonso have another electric fire if he likes. The bathroom's next door, by the way — all nice and modern, look.

Anne: Mm. . . yes, that's OK. Now, about the rent. I think you said it was £150 per month?

Landlord: That's right — and I'll need £100 deposit as soon as he decides, of course.

Anne: Right. Well, thanks very much, Mr Lamb. I'll get Carlos to give you a ring as soon as he makes up his mind.

Now complete Anne's notes and finish her message to Carlos.

Carlos

Saw flat in Fulham Road
last night.
Details as follows:
LIVING ROOM
Quite large. Gets plenty of
sunshine. Good, thick walls so
noise no problem. Heating by
electric fire. Paraffin heater
in attic if necessary. Could be
cold in winter.
KITCHEN
BEDROOM
BATHROOM
RENT
NB Seems quite reasonable for
area. If interested, phone
landlord (898 7654) as soon
as you get back.

Written tasks

1   You have invited friends to stay in your house for two weeks while
you are on holiday. Write the message you leave for them, giving them
all the information they need about the house and the area. Use the
model message at the beginning of this unit to help you, and include
some of these ideas:

— food. Where are the best shops? Is anything delivered to the
house?
— sheets and blankets. Where are they kept?
— instructions about heating/TV/other equipment.
— the garden. Does it need watering?
— any pets to be fed?
— places to visit nearby?
— local transport?

2   You feel ill, so you are leaving work early. Write some notes about
what you were planning to do, so that a colleague can deal with any
important work for you.

UNIT 6

Describing a person

The Beatles as they were in 1963.

Anne is a keen pop music fan. She gets a regular weekly magazine which profiles different pop stars each month. On this occasion, the profile is of Paul McCartney.

MAGGIE DEAN MEETS PAUL McCARTNEY

EXCLUSIVE!

I first saw Paul McCartney twenty years ago, when, as a birthday present, I was given two tickets for a Beatles concert. I have been a fan ever since. So, when my editor sent me to do an interview with Paul, I was, of course, delighted. I was also rather curious to see what sort of man he is after so many years as a superstar.

Probably the most surprising thing about Paul is that he never seems to get any older. He's a tallish, slim, fit-looking man, extremely alert, and now in his early forties. He's got dark, wavy hair and an open, boyish, often playful expression. He arrived for our interview dressed in blue denim jeans and an open-neck striped shirt. Strangely, he looked rather shy.

To me, he seems a natural, down-to-earth sort of man. He is very happily married and lives with his wife, Linda, and four children in the south of England. Most days, he travels up to his London office, where he works hard writing songs, giving interviews and making hit records. Compared with many other superstars who let money and fame destroy their lives, Paul McCartney must consider himself a very lucky man.

Notes

The description above is divided into three paragraphs.

1 What information are we given in the first paragraph of the description? In what ways does this information make a suitable introduction?

2 What information are we given in the second paragraph? How is it different from the final paragraph?

31

Word search

Find words in the text which correspond to the following:

quite tall — lively/wide-awake
in good condition physically — wearing blue jeans
a man aged 40–45 — sensible/practical
hair which is not straight

Useful adjectives

'Computer Penfriends' has promised to find you a penfriend. You must supply the necessary information to feed into the computer. Choose the qualities you prefer from the following:

short/tall — shy/out-going
slim/well-built/of medium build — ambitious/easy-going
dark hair/fair hair — friendly/reserved
curly hair/straight hair — kind/tactless
serious/fun-loving — cheerful/moody
adventurous/home-loving — in his/her early teens/
quiet/talkative — twenties/thirties

2 Which of the above adjectives could you use to describe the person sitting next to you? Make a list and then see if he/she agrees with you.

3 Can you add any more descriptive adjectives to the list? Write them down and then compare your list with the rest of the class.

Hyphenated adjectives

> He was a well-built, broad-shouldered man.

Look at the box above, then change the following sentences in the same way.

Example: a man with dark hair — *He's a dark-haired man*.

1 a man with a bad temper
2 a girl with long hair
3 a man with a deep voice
4 a boy with round shoulders
5 a woman who dresses well

Order of adjectives

> Our teacher was a tallish, well-built, broad-shouldered man. He was a middle-aged, Mexican gentleman.

We put nationalities and colours just in front of the noun.
(an *English* girl; a *blue* book)

Before these, we put adjectives which give the facts.
(a *little*, blue book; a *thick*, English dictionary)

Before both of these, we put adjectives which give our judgement. (a *pretty*, little, Spanish child; a *horrible*, large, hairy spider)

If there is no other difference between the adjectives, we put the shorter one first. (a *tall*, long-legged girl; a *large*, heavy book)

Put the following adjectives in the correct order:

1 He was an / English / attractive / young / man.
2 It was a / boring / green / little / book.
3 She is a / Colombian / hard-working / quiet / student.
4 She was dressed in a / full-length / beautiful / evening dress.
5 She's got brown / beautiful / big / eyes.

Descriptions

1 Write a few lines describing each of the people in the pictures below. Describe each picture accurately, but use your imagination too. The first description has been done for you.

Example: *He's a well-built man of medium height and is probably in his late twenties. He's got longish, straight, dark hair and brown eyes. He's dressed in a lightweight, grey suit, white shirt, blue and white, striped tie and black shoes. He looks rather depressed.*

2 Now stand back to back with your partner. Try to describe him/her accurately without turning round. Your partner will tell you if you are right or wrong as you go along.

Written tasks

1 Use the prompts below to build up a description of a student. Before you begin, think about the tenses you will use.

Last month / I / join / evening class / because / want / learn / English. First day / I / be / curious / see / what / other students / like. When / I / enter / classroom / I / notice / one / student / particular. We / now / good friends / and / we / often / meet / evenings.

   My neighbour's name / Manuela. She / tall / slim / Italian girl, / early twenties. She / big / brown / eyes / and / friendly / smile. She / usually / wear / blue jeans / but / today / dressed / skirt / blouse.

   Although / she / serious / student, / she / lively / imaginative / and / have / good / sense of humour. She / like / sport / and / be / excellent / dancer. I / hope / we / not lose touch / each other / when / course / finish.

2 Using the language you have practised in this unit, describe someone in your class/office/work. When you have finished, show your description to the person you described and see what they think.

3 Describe someone who is well known on television or in the cinema. Do not give his/her name and see if other people in your class can guess who you have described.

UNIT 7

Giving instructions

Susan lives in a block of flats near a college. A lot of foreign students come to London in summer to study at the college for a short time. To help new students, the following set of instructions has been placed in the college call box.

PLEASE READ THESE INSTRUCTIONS CAREFULLY!

To make a call you will need 10p pieces. Make sure you know the
dialling code for the town you are calling, unless it is a local call.

TO OPERATE THE TELEPHONE

First, lift the receiver and listen for the dialling tone.
Next, dial the number you require, beginning with the code for that
area. You should hear a ringing tone.
Wait until you hear rapid pips. This means your call has been answered.
Insert your money in the slot.
If the rapid pips are repeated before you have finished your call, insert
more money.

EMERGENCIES

Call the operator by dialling 999.
Tell the operator the emergency service you want (Fire, Police or Ambulance),
and your telephone number.
Wait until the emergency authority answers.
Then give them the address where help is needed.

Notes

A Remember written instructions must be clear. For this reason, they tend to consist of short, simple sentences. Each instruction is usually placed on a new line. Imperative forms of the verb are most commonly used for this sort of writing.

B The following words are sometimes used when giving instructions. Check that you know how to use them.

First, . . .	After that, . . .
Then/Next, . . .	Avoid (-ing) . . .
Make sure you . . .	Take care not to . . .
Remember to . . .	Do not . . .
As soon as . . . . . . , you should . . .	

Interpreting instructions

What would you do if a child in your care tipped a saucepan full of boiling water off the cooker and onto his legs?

The pictures and instructions below come from a First Aid book and outline the correct way to treat a scald (a burn caused by hot liquid or steam). Neither the pictures nor the instructions are in the correct order. Work with a partner to match them together and then write out the instructions in the correct order, as you would expect to find them in a First Aid leaflet.

HOW TO TREAT A SCALD

- When these have been removed, lay the casualty down.

- Finally, if the scald is serious, arrange for the casualty to be taken to hospital.

- Then, quickly remove anything tight like rings, boots or belts, before the parts start to swell.

- Cover the burnt area with a clean, dry cloth or dressing.

- First, place the burnt area in cool water for at least ten minutes.

Oral instructions

1 Look back to the model instructions on using the telephone at the beginning of this unit and notice how the Imperative form of the verb is used.

2 Now tell your partner how to perform *one* of these activities:
— do a series of yoga/keep fit exercises
— make a cup of tea
— use a cassette recorder.

USEFUL VOCABULARY		
YOGA/KEEP FIT	A CUP OF TEA	CASSETTE RECORDER
to bend	to boil	to insert a cassette
to lean	to fill	to press a button
to lie/sit down	to pour	to switch on/off
to stretch	to warm	play/stop/fast forward/
to touch	a kettle	rewind/buttons
	a teabag	
	a teapot	
	a teaspoon(ful)	

Written instructions

With your partner, complete the hotel notice telling guests what to do in case of fire. The illustrations may give you some ideas.

FIRE NOTICE

As soon as you find your room, ... If you see smoke or flames, ...
....
If you hear the fire bell... .... where one of the staff will be waiting to check that you are safe.

Written tasks

1

Use the prompts below to build up a set of written instructions.

HOW TO OPERATE A WASHING MACHINE

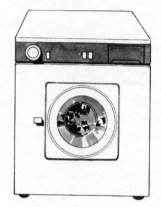

First / sort / dirty washing / piles.
Then / load / clothes / machine. Take care /
  not / overload / machine.
Select / programme / require.
Fill / appropriate / compartment / washing
  powder.
Make sure / not / use / too much powder!
Close / door / carefully / press / red
  button.
Not / attempt / open / door / until /
  programme / be / completed!
As soon as / machine / stop, / remove /
  clothes / prevent /creasing.

VOCABULARY

to load
  to put clothes into
  the machine
to overload
  to put too many
  clothes into the
  machine
to select
  to choose
to prevent
  to stop

2

Write a set of instructions for a coffee/drinks machine.

3

Choose a favourite meal of yours which is easy to cook and write a list of instructions. Use the vocabulary in the box to help you. You may like to ask a friend to try your recipe, to see if it works.

USEFUL VOCABULARY

to chop / peel / slice
to beat / mix / stir
to bake / boil / fry /
  grill / roast

Giving directions

It's Anne's birthday on Friday and she and Susan are planning to have a party. Susan is writing some invitations.

Notes

1 Do you remember where to put the address on a friendly letter? And your name?

2 What information is given in each paragraph of the letter?

3 What is the purpose of the first and the final paragraph?

4 Which form of the verbs shown below do we most commonly use to give instructions/ directions?

a) You are turning left.
b) Turn left.
c) You must turn left.

17 Enfield Court,
Enfield Road,
Twickenham,
Middlesex
16th August 1986

Dear Sean,

I'm writing to invite you to a party we're having at the flat next Friday, August 22nd. As you know, it's Anne's 21st birthday next week and my birthday next month, so we thought we'd celebrate together and have a joint party.

I can't remember if you've been round to the flat before, but anyway, if you follow the directions below, you shouldn't get lost.

Take the Number 15 bus from the station and get off at the Star Hotel. Walk down Cromwell Road, past the Odeon Cinema, and then take the first turning on the right. That's Sandy Road. Turn left at the first junction, then go straight past the church as far as the next crossroads. Turn right and our block of flats is the second on the right (see map below).

Do try and come - it seems ages since we last had a chat. Of course you're welcome to bring someone with you if you want to.

Look forward to seeing you then!

Love,
Sue

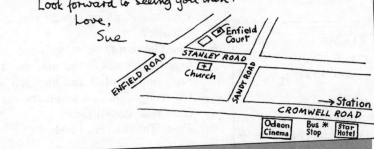

Future plans

We're having a party next Friday.

Remember that we often use the Present Continuous tense when speaking about future plans. Use the following prompts to interview your neighbour about his/her future arrangements.

You/go/out/this evening?
You/do/anything special/this weekend?
When/you/take/holiday/this year? Where/you/go?
How/you/get/home/tonight?
You/come/school dance/Saturday?

Giving directions

Look at the map and read the conversation.

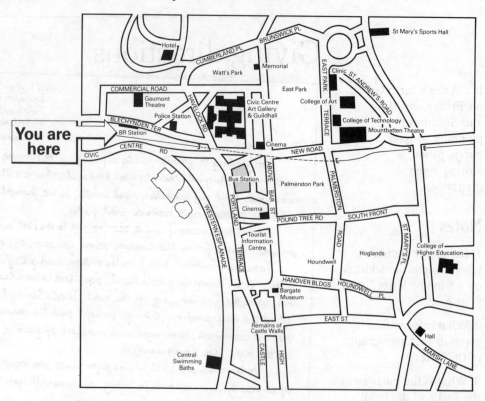

A: Excuse me, please, could you tell me the way to the Gaumont Theatre?

B: The Gaumont? Now, let's see . . . Yes, go along this road, bearing left where the road divides. When you get to the T-junction, turn left and then left again. That's Commercial Road. Go straight on and you'll see the Gaumont on your left. You can't miss it. All right?

A: Fine. Thanks very much.

USEFUL LANGUAGE

Go along . . . . . .
   until you reach
   . . .
Go as far as . . . . . .
   and then . . .
Go straight on / over /
   across / past . . .
Turn left / right at . . .
Take the first
   (turning) on your
   left.
Bear left / right.
a crossing
a footpath
a one-way street
a roundabout
a T-junction
traffic lights
a subway
a zebra crossing

1

Practise with a partner the conversation shown above and then work out similar exchanges. Use the language in the box to help you.

You are at the railway station. Ask your partner how to get to:

a the College of Art
b the bus station
c the cinema
d the Central Swimming Baths
e the hotel

2

Complete the sentences with an appropriate preposition or phrase:

Take the number 10 bus _____ Victoria coach station and get ____ _____ the cinema. Walk back _____ Church Road, go straight _____ the roundabout and take the second turning _____ the left. Go straight on, _____ the church and the park, _____ _____ _____ the traffic lights. You will see a little footpath _____ your left. Go _____ the footpath and my house is right _____ _____ _____ you. You can't miss it!

3

Draw a rough map of the area where you live, including the main road, bus stop, and your street. Tell your partner how to get to your home from the centre of town.

Written tasks

1 Use the following prompts to build up a letter of invitation:

20 Cypress Avenue,
Wenton,
Warwickshire.

16th May 1986

Dear Maggie,
    I / write / apologise / not / write / sooner / and / ask / if you / like / come / dinner / Saturday. As you know we / move / new house last week / so we / think / we / like / have / small house-warming party.
    I / enclose / little map / area / help you. As you / see house / very near / station. When you / come out / station / turn right / right again. Take / first / turning / left. That / be / Cypress Avenue. Our house / be / nearly / end / road, / just beside / new block / flats.
    I hope / you / come. You already know / all / other guests / so / it should be / lovely evening.
    Look forward / hear / all your news !
              Love,

             Rebecca

2 Write a letter, inviting a friend to a party at your house/flat. Enclose a map and directions on how to reach you.

UNIT 9

Writing a narrative

To start you thinking:

How often have you travelled by air?

Do you enjoy flying?

Have you ever had any interesting/frightening experiences while flying?

As an air hostess, Anne takes a special interest in stories about flying. This story, from a weekly magazine, really made her think!

READERS' PAGE 'FLY? I'D RATHER STAY AT HOME'

Businessman David Lamb explains why he now thinks twice before travelling by plane.

July 14th 1982 is a day I shall never forget. On that day, I stared death in the face.

Our flight was due to leave at 11 am that day, and I arrived at the airport with plenty of time to spare. We started boarding at 10.30. Most of us were holiday-makers and there was a lot of laughing and joking going on. It was raining slightly, but visibility was good, and the plane took off on time. The cabin staff were just beginning to bring round the duty-free goods, when the plane began to shake.

At first we thought we had just hit bad weather. We were told to sit down and to fasten our seat belts. Then, suddenly, the front of the plane seemed to dip, and we realised we were speeding towards the ground. People screamed in panic. Strangers joined hands and prayed. We all thought we had only minutes to live.

Then, just when we had given up all hope, we felt the plane level out, and slowly we began to gain height. A few minutes later, the pilot announced that everything was now under control, and we all began to clap and cheer hysterically. Twenty minutes later, we landed safely. Experts are still investigating the cause of the incident, but until now they have found no real answers. As for me, I shall never feel really safe on a plane again. It was the most frightening experience of my life.

Notes

Remember that a good story should have the following features:

— an interesting beginning, which attracts the reader's attention and makes him want to read on.

— a well thought-out development. Events should follow each other in a logical order. Start a new paragraph for each new stage in the story.

— a good ending. Always leave yourself plenty of time for this — there is nothing worse than reading an exciting story which just stops in mid-air!

1 This story is divided into four paragraphs. Which stage of the events is covered in each of these paragraphs?

2 Do you think the first paragraph provides a good introduction to the story? Why/Why not?

Word search

Find words in the text which correspond to the following:

getting on the plane   going very fast
the plane left   to ask God for help
to incline downwards   with uncontrolled emotion

Narrative tenses

Look back to the story at the beginning of the unit and note all the past tense forms. How many forms can you find?

THE PAST CONTINUOUS TENSE (was -ing)

1 Look back to the second paragraph of the story and notice how the writer uses the Past Continuous tense to describe what was happening *before* anything unusual was noticed. (It was raining./ People were laughing and joking.)

2 Study the picture below. It shows the scene on a beach just before a shark attack. Complete the paragraph. It describes what was going on before the shark was seen. Use the Past Continuous tense where possible. Use the vocabulary in the box on the left to help you.

USEFUL VOCABULARY

to fish
to make sandcastles
to paddle
to relax
to sunbathe
to swim
a bucket and spade
a motor boat
rockpools
rocks
seaweed
a swimmer
shallow/deep water

I remember everything vividly. It was just an ordinary summer afternoon and the beach was crowded. People . . . . Some very small children . . . . . . while their parents looked on. Other children . . . . . . or . . . . Off shore, some young people . . . . . . while a short distance away . . . . . . .Then we heard the scream!

43

THE SIMPLE PAST

1 Look back again to the story at the beginning of this unit and notice how in the third paragraph the writer uses the Simple Past tense to describe what happened *after* the plane began to shake. Notice that the use of very short sentences makes the story even more dramatic.

2 Study the beach scene again and imagine the shark has just been seen. Complete the next paragraph of the story. It describes what happened *after* the shark was seen. Use the Simple Past tense where possible. Use the vocabulary in the box on the left to help you.

USEFUL VOCABULARY

to dash
to point to
to scream in panic
to shout
to stare/gaze in
   horror
desperately

At first everything seemed to go very quiet. Then, everyone jumped to their feet. They . . . . . . at the black fin, now clearly visible. The people in the water . . . . On the beach, mothers and fathers . . . . The children who had been playing on the beach . . . . . . Seconds later, a coastguard . . . . . . and . . . . The shark . . . . Everybody held their breath.

Linking events

They were just bringing round the duty-free goods when the plane began to shake. *At first* we thought we had hit bad weather. *Then*, the front of the plane began to dip. *Seconds/minutes later*, we realised we were speeding towards the ground.

In the stories below, events are in the wrong order. In pairs, decide on the correct order. Then write short paragraphs, linking the events in the way shown in the box above.

A ROAD ACCIDENT

Another motorist arrived and ran to phone for an ambulance.
He just stared at them in shock, wondering what to do.
He pulled himself together and ran to check that nobody was seriously injured.
John was standing at the corner when he saw the cars crash into each other.

A BURGLARY

She thought the cat had knocked something over downstairs.
Mrs Thompson was trying to get to sleep when she heard the sound of breaking glass.
She realised there was someone moving about in the kitchen, below her.
She heard the sound of footsteps on the stairs.

Discussion

It is easiest to write a story based on personal experience. Close your eyes and think of the most frightening experience of your life. Now ask each other about that experience, using the prompts below. Make sure you use the correct tense.

1 Ask about the background. (What was happening before the incident.)
When/happen? Where/be/you? Anyone/with you?
What/you/do/at the time? And the other people?

2 Ask about the event itself.
What/happen? How/you/feel? What/you/do/next?
What/other people/do? What/happen/afterwards?

3 Ask about later developments.
How/you/feel/now/when/remember/incident? You/ever/dream about it? It/change/your life/in any way?

Written tasks

1 Use the prompts below to build up a narrative about a hotel fire.

Last year / I / spend / summer holidays / popular resort / Mediterranean coast. Hotel / be / modern / comfortable / and / weather / perfect. I / have marvellous / holiday — until / fire!

It / be / Saturday evening / and / everybody / relax / in / lounge / or / discotheque / tired / after / long day / beach. The disco / be / ground floor / hotel / and / this Saturday night / it / be / crowded with people / dance / and / drink. Disc jockey / play / old Beatles hits / from / 60s / and / people / sing along / and / generally / have / good time. Then / suddenly / we / smell / smoke!

First / only / few people / notice / fire. Then / as clouds / black smoke / begin / fill / room / everybody / start / shout / scream / panic. People / race / exits. One fire door / be / locked / and / people / turn back / frantically / and / join / crowds / other exits. Everyone / begin / cough / choke.

Then / just as / we / think / we / never / escape / help / arrive. Firemen / fight / way / into / room / and / soon / everyone / be / safely / out of / building. Luckily / nobody / be / seriously / hurt. Holiday company / offer us / rooms / another hotel / nearby / but / my holiday / be / spoilt / and I / fly / home / next day. I / not be / inside / discotheque / since then. It / be / most frightening experience / my life!

2 Using the ideas you gathered in the Discussion exercise, write a narrative entitled *The most frightening experience of my life*. Remember to start new paragraphs for the background, for the event itself, and for describing later developments.

3 You were on your way home from work one day when you witnessed a serious accident. Describe how the accident happened and what you did to help.

Giving a speech or a talk

The airline Anne works for is giving a staff party. One of the stewards, Jim, is leaving the airline today, so Anne has been asked to make a farewell speech.

A speech

"Just a minute, everybody. Could I have your attention please! I think you all know that it's Jim's last day with the airline today and I've been asked to say a few words, on behalf of all of us here. I'm not used to making speeches so I'll try to keep it short!

As you know, Jim has decided to give up flying and take up a new career in business. Well, we're all going to miss him very much after all this time, and I think we'd all like to thank him for being such a nice person to work with. Speaking for myself, I shall always remember what good fun we had together while we were working on long-distance flights. There are lots of stories I could tell about that, but I'd better keep them for another occasion!

Anyway, Jim, we all wish you lots of luck for the future— and on behalf of everybody here, I'd like to give you this little present. We hope it will remind you of us in years to come!"

Notes

A There are many ways of making a speech, depending on where you are and how formal the situation is. It is important to consider carefully *who* you are speaking to (a small friendly crowd / a large formal audience?) and *why* you are speaking (giving information / congratulating someone / saying goodbye?). The language used for a formal wedding may be different from that used at a small office party. For example:

FORMAL	INFORMAL
Good evening, ladies and gentlemen, could I have your attention please.	Just a minute, everybody, could I have your attention, please.
We'd like to present you with this little gift.	We'd like to give you this little present.
I'd like to finish by saying . . .	Well, I think that's about all I wanted to say.

OTHER USEFUL LANGUAGE

The most formal language is marked with an asterisk(*). The other language could be used in both formal and informal situations.

> * Good afternoon/evening, everybody and thank you for coming.
> I'd like to tell you something about . . .
> As you know, we're here today to . . .
> * I'd like to take this opportunity to congratulate/thank/tell you . . .
> On behalf of us all . . .
> We'd like to wish you . . .
> Speaking for myself, I . . .
> * Thank you for being such an attentive audience.

B Read Anne's speech again and answer the following questions:

1 How many paragraphs are there in the speech? What is the function of each of the paragraphs?
2 Where is the speech being made? Do you think it is a formal/informal party? Why?
3 Remember that a speech is something to be said/read aloud. Can you find any words or phrases in the text which show that Anne is actually *speaking* to an audience?
4 Pick out any words or phrases not mentioned in the boxes above, which might be useful when writing a speech.

Word search

Find words in the text which correspond to the following:

as the representative of everybody here	a new profession
	we'll feel sad he's not with us
not accustomed to	for another (more suitable) time
to stop	a present/something given

Prepositions

> We'd like to thank you *for* being such a nice person.

Look at the box above, then complete the sentences below with the appropriate preposition.

1 We wanted to congratulate you _____ your promotion.
2 I'd like to tell you something _____ my country.
3 On behalf of us all, may I present you _____ this gift.
4 We'd like to wish you good luck _____ the future. (*two possibilities*)
5 I'd like to finish _____ saying how delighted I am to receive this gift.
6 We're depending _____ you for our future support.

The 'going to' future

> We're all going to miss him.

Remember that we use the 'going to' future to speak about things we intend to do in the future. Make questions from the following prompts and then interview your neighbour.

Where/you/spend/your next holiday?
You/continue/learning English after this course?
You/read/any English books or newspapers/this week?
When/you/do/homework?
You/go/watch/TV/tonight/or/you/go/out?

Gerund or Infinitive?

Work in pairs to complete the sentences below. Supply the correct preposition, and then the appropriate form of the verb. Remember that your English dictionary should give you the necessary information, if you are in doubt.

1 I'm not accustomed _____ (speak) in public.
2 He's decided to take _____ (teach).
3 We'd like to thank you _____ (take) so much trouble.
4 I'd like _____ (give) you this little gift.
5 We look forward _____ (see) you at our next reunion.
6 Are you planning _____ (stay) in London?
7 We want _____ (wish) you lots of luck.
8 Do you remember when you used _____ (work) with us in the Accounts Office?
9 Congratulations _____ (pass) your examinations.
10 (Speak) _____ myself, I will find it very strange here without you.

Written tasks

1 Use the prompts below to build up Jim's speech of thanks at the airline party.

66 Well, everybody/I/just like/take this opportunity/thank you/this lovely gift/and/your good wishes.
   As/think/you/know/I/work here/eight years now/and/I/really/enjoy/work/with such/nice group/people. I/really/go/miss/you all/but/hope/be able/come back/see you again soon.
   Anyway/I/think/that/be all I want/say/ — except I/like/thank you again/behalf/myself and my wife/lovely gift and wish/you/many more years/happy flying! 99

2 It is the end of term and you are having a celebration party. One of your teachers is leaving the school. Write the speech of farewell which you give at the party.

A talk

Susan recently attended a meeting where a guest speaker had been invited to give a short talk on Oxfam.

> Well, good morning everybody and thank you all for coming here today in spite of the terrible weather. I know you have a lot of other business to deal with, so I'll be very brief.
>
> As you know, I've come here today to tell you something about our work at Oxfam. Oxfam is a charity which tries to help people all over the world who are suffering from hunger or poverty or the effects of a disaster. We depend on ordinary people like you to raise money for our projects — in this way we can send food to victims of disaster or send experts to give training in medicine, agriculture and engineering. Since the charity was started in 1942, the lives of many thousands of people have been saved in this way. As you probably know, there are Oxfam shops throughout the country which raise money by selling things given to us by helpers. There are also local groups of volunteers who help in many ways to keep the charity going. We always need more help, and if anybody here is interested in knowing more, please don't hesitate to come forward.
>
> Well, I think that's all I wanted to say in general, but I will be here at the front of the hall to answer any questions and to take the names of volunteers. Thank you all for being so attentive.

Notes

A Notice that the language used for giving a talk is very similar to that used for making speeches. Can you find examples of this language in the talk above?

B When you give a talk it is usual to:

— greet your audience and introduce yourself.
— tell your audience what you are going to speak about.
— give detailed information about your subject.
— show with a suitable phrase that you have nearly finished your talk.
— invite anyone with questions to stay.
— thank your audience.

Transfer

In groups, prepare a talk which one of you will give to the whole class. You may like to speak about a charity, a hobby or a place you have visited. Use the talk above and the Notes on this page and pages 46 and 47 to help you.

Written task

Prepare a talk to give to the whole class on *either* some aspect of life in your country *or* a recent holiday which you greatly enjoyed.

Outlining advantages and disadvantages

Anne's niece, Jane, is thinking of applying for a job as an air hostess. She has written to Anne to ask how she finds the job and whether she would recommend it to others. This is Anne's reply.

Notes

A

When setting out the advantages and disadvantages of a topic, it is important to make a clear plan before you begin. It is a good idea to note down points for and against the subject as you think of them; you can decide on the correct order later on.

B

There are five paragraphs in Anne's letter. What information are we given in each of the paragraphs?

C

Does Anne recommend flying as a career? How does she make this clear?

D

Some examples of useful language are shown in the box on the right.

---

17 Enfield Court,
Enfield Road,
Twickenham,
Middlesex MV6 3PQ

6th April 1986

Dear Jane,

I was delighted to get your letter, and to hear that you've passed all your exams. Congratulations! You must have worked very hard to get such good results!

In your letter you ask if I would recommend flying as a career. Perhaps if I tell you one or two of the advantages and the disadvantages of the job, it might help you to make a decision.

For me, one of the biggest advantages is that you have the opportunity to travel all round the world, and to visit places you would probably never see otherwise. Your colleagues are usually quite young and you can have great fun getting round and seeing the sights together. What's more, you can get very cheap travel for yourself and your family, which means that you can have some fantastic holidays at very low prices.

There are some disadvantages, of course, as in all jobs. The work can be pretty hard physically, and you need to be fit and healthy and to have a good strong pair of feet! Also, while most passengers are extremely pleasant, you do sometimes get some difficult ones who are never satisfied with the service. If you've already got jet-lag and sore feet, they can really test your patience!

All things considered, though, I think the good points far outweigh the bad, and I have certainly enjoyed my two years flying. Anyway, if you do decide to apply, please don't hesitate to write to me again and let me know if I can help in any way.

Looking forward to hearing from you soon,

Love,

Anne

For me / As I see it, one of the biggest advantages / disadvantages of (X) is that . . .
Also, / Added to this, / What is more, / Furthermore, . . .
All things considered / To sum up then, I think . . .

Word search   Find words or phrases in the text which correspond with the
following:

very pleased   really enjoy yourself
a job/profession   quite
to decide   in good athletic condition
people you work with   are of much more importance

**Linking
sentences**

Most passengers are extremely pleasant *but* you can also
get difficult ones.
Although most passengers are extremely pleasant, you
can also get difficult ones.
While most passengers are extremely pleasant, you can
also get difficult ones.

We use words like *although* and *while* to link contrasting ideas on
the same topic.

Flying can be great fun. *However*, there are some
disadvantages.
Flying can be great fun. *On the other hand*, there are
some disadvantages.

Words like *however* and *on the other hand* are used to introduce an
opposite point.

You have the opportunity to travel all round the world.
You can *also* get very cheap travel for yourself and your family.

You have the opportunity to travel all round the world.
What is more,/Furthermore, you can get very cheap
travel for yourself and your family.

We use words like *also*, *what is more* and *furthermore* to add more
points on a topic.

Study the boxes above and then complete the following sentences:

1 While travelling by air is quick, . . .
2 A camping holiday is cheap. Furthermore, . . .
3 If you live in a city there's plenty to do. On the other hand, . . .
4 Although learning a foreign language can be very hard work, . . .
5 Cars are very expensive to buy. What's more, . . .

Writing paragraphs

Remember that a paragraph usually consists of a number of sentences which deal with *one* aspect or stage of your discussion/story. Remember also that a paragraph should start on a new line, a little way in from the margin.

The sentences below should form two separate paragraphs but they have been mixed together. In pairs, decide which points should be grouped together and then write out the two separate paragraphs. The first sentence of each paragraph has been printed in *italic*.

- What is more, television can have a serious educational side and there are plenty of good current affairs programmes and documentaries which are very informative.

- While it is good to have such cheap and convenient entertainment in your own living room, it may also mean the end of reading and conversation for large parts of the evening.

- Furthermore, although there are many good programmes on television, there is often far too much blood and violence on the screen.

- *One of the most obvious advantages of having a television is that it offers cheap and convenient entertainment which nearly everyone can afford.*

- This can be especially harmful for children, who will often sit up late watching horror films and then have nightmares for days afterwards.

- *On the other hand, having a television can have certain disadvantages.*

- This is especially important for people who are alone all day, or for large families who can't afford to go out to cinemas and theatres.

Planning what to write

In pairs, note down some points for and against one of these topics:
— owning a car
— being an only child

You should list at least three advantages and three disadvantages. Compare your ideas with those of other members of the class.

Written tasks

1   Using the notes you made in the previous exercise, write a composition outlining the advantages and disadvantages of *either* owning a car *or* being an only child.

Use the plan below as a guide.

Paragraph one

> **General introduction**: State if you have any personal experience of this subject. Say if you have heard or read any recent articles/stories which are relevant to this subject.

Paragraph two

> List two or three advantages. (Remember to link your ideas together.)

Paragraph three

> List two or three disadvantages.

Paragraph four

> **Conclusion**: State whether in your opinion the advantages outweigh the disadvantages or not.

2   Write a composition outlining the advantages and disadvantages of living *either* in a foreign country *or* in a city.

Writing notices and advertisements

These are some of the advertisements and notices which appeared on the college noticeboard last week.

Wanted

Third person to share large central flat. Own room. £25.00 including bills.
Contact: Angela Smith
Tel: 898-7264

KEEP FIT CLASSES

LOOK GOOD - FEEL GREAT!

Daytime Classes

Monday 2 - 2.45 pm
(Swimming available
    after class)
Friday 11 - 12 am

Evening Classes

Monday 6.30 - 7.15 pm

SPECIAL OFFER!

First visit - bring a
friend and two can
enter for the price
of one!

ALL CLASSES £1.20

FOR SALE

LADY'S BICYCLE

PERFECT CONDITION

RING 894-0996

SAFARI TO INDIA - THIRD PERSON REQUIRED

We are looking for someone to join us on a minibus safari to India, leaving in April.

Are you: - aged 20-25?

- fit and healthy?

- an experienced driver?

- able to keep calm in a crisis?

- mechanically minded?

- prepared for tough conditions?

If so, you could be just the person we're looking for!

DATES	Depart mid-April. Return end of August.
COST	£700 basic (plus spending money as required).
EQUIPMENT	You will need a lightweight tent, sleeping bag and cooking utensils.
INTERESTED?	If you would like more details contact:

Jane Bruce,
16 West Way,
London EC3 9EA
Tel: (01)-634-8922

Notes

A

Remember that a notice or advertisement must be easy to read. Information is grouped under precise headings such as *For sale, Wanted, Lost.* Above all, a notice should be concise. Be careful that you do not confuse the reader by giving too much information.

B

Notice that we often use note form (see Unit 5) when writing a short notice/advertisement.

Short notices

1 Look again at the short notices/advertisements. Can you say exactly what they mean?

2 In groups, write short notices for the school/office for the following items:

1 You want to sell a bicycle. Give a description and say how much you want for it.
2 You are looking for someone to share your flat. Give details of the flat, the rent, and who to contact.
3 You found a watch lying in the street. Say exactly where and when you found it, describe the watch, and say how the owner can reclaim it.

3 Compare your notices/advertisements with those of other groups.

Longer notices

1 Study the notice entitled *Safari to India*. Notice again how information is grouped under separate headings such as *Dates*, *Cost*, *Equipment*.

2 Now read the conversation below between John and Liz. They both work at the Royal London Hospital, Richmond. The hospital needs a new kidney machine and John and Liz are trying to think of ways to raise enough money to buy one.

Liz: Hey, John, I've got an idea! Why don't we organise a swimarathon?

John: A swimarathon? What on earth's that?

Liz: Oh, haven't you heard of it before? Well, it's a charity swim. You need teams of six people who take it in turns to swim a length of the swimming pool. Each swimmer has to find sponsors, you know, people who promise to pay him some money for every length he swims — 10p a length is usual. Then, on the day, each team swims as many lengths as possible in one hour. The more lengths they swim, the more money they raise.

John: Hey, that's a great idea! Now, where could we do it?

Liz: Well, what about Manor Road Swimming Baths? I'm sure they'd let us use their facilities.

John: Fine! What about the date? Saturday would be the best day, of course — maybe the last Saturday in April — the 23rd?

Liz: OK. Look, why don't we write a notice to put up in the Baths, asking for volunteers — you know — saying the money is for the kidney machine, and that anyone can take part as long as they can swim a few lengths.

John: Good idea! We could give the hospital number — it's 69876, I think — and ask the receptionist, Angela Johnson, to look after the inquiries.

Liz: Right! Come on then. Let's think how to write this notice!

3 Using the information given in the dialogue on the previous page, work with a partner to complete the notice below:

```
        VOLUNTEERS NEEDED FOR SWIMARATHON

The Royal London Hospital is desperately in need of a

new ...... . To help raise the necessary money, we are

organising a ...... and we are looking for teams of

...... . Each team will have to find people to ......

them. Don't worry if you are not a marvellous ......,

as long as you can swim ......, you can take part.

PLACE ......

DATE ......

Will you help? For more details contact:

        ............

        Tel: ......

REMEMBER With your help we can ...... .

        Please give us your support!
```

Transfer

In groups, write a notice headed *New members needed for local club.*

Give a short description of the club and what you do.
State whether new members need any previous experience or not.
Give details of weekly/monthly meetings including place, time etc.
Give the name and telephone number of the person to be contacted for information.

Written tasks

1 You are organising a trip to a theatre/football match/pop festival or some other such event. Write a notice giving details of the trip including date, times, means of transport, programme etc.

2 Write three short advertisements for your school/office noticeboard under the headings a) *Wanted* b) *Lost!* c) *For sale.*

UNIT 13

Describing festivals and ceremonies

To start you thinking: Which festival in your country do you enjoy most?
What happens during the festival?

Do you know about any special days or festivals celebrated in Great Britain? How much do you know about them?

NOTTING HILL CARNIVAL

Notting Hill Carnival is held in London each August Bank Holiday, and is the largest and most colourful street event in Britain. The festival celebrates the traditions of the British black community who emigrated to Great Britain from the West Indies in the 1950s. They brought with them the Caribbean idea of 'carnival', with processions, colourful costumes, steel bands and street dancing.

Preparations for the carnival begin many months beforehand. Costumes have to be made, and floats built, ready for the street procession. Steel bands practise traditional Caribbean music on instruments made from old oil drums. Shortly before the festival, the streets are

decorated with red, green and yellow streamers, and amplifiers are set in place, to carry the rhythmic sounds over the roar of the London traffic.

The carnival lasts for three days, and is full of music and colour. Processions of floats, steel and brass bands, and dancers in exotic costumes make their way through the narrow London streets, watched by thousands of people. The streets are lined with stalls selling tropical fruits, such as fresh pineapple, water melons and mangoes. Everybody dances — black and white, young and old — even the policemen on duty take part in the fun. For these three days in August, a little Caribbean magic touches the streets of London.

Notes

A Each paragraph in the article describes a different aspect of the festival. What information are we given in each paragraph?

B The Passive is often used when describing festivals and other such events. Find examples of this in the article.

C Festivals are usually regular annual events. What verb tenses should be used to describe such events?

Word search   Find words in the text which correspond to the following:

left their country
a line of people moving
  through the streets
in advance

a vehicle decorated for a street
  procession
oil containers
paper decorations
a table used for selling goods

Passives

> Costumes have to be made.
> Streets are decorated with streamers.

Look at the examples above and then change the following sentences into the more impersonal Passive form:

1 People usually cook a special meal in the evening.
2 They perform traditional dances.
3 They must wear national costume.
4 People often exchange gifts.
5 People usually begin preparations some weeks beforehand.

Prepositions   Complete the sentences with an appropriate preposition:

1 The streets are decorated _____ streamers.
2 The dancers make their way _____ the narrow London streets.
3 The streets are lined _____ stalls selling tropical fruits.
4 The procession is watched _____ thousands of people.
5 Many West Indians came to Britain _____ the 1950s.
6 Thousands of people take part _____ the celebrations.
7 The carnival is held _____ August.
8 The dancers are dressed _____ colourful costumes.
9 The instruments are made _____ old oil drums.
10 It is the largest street event _____ Europe.

Vocabulary practice   Make adjectives from the following nouns.

Example: care — *careful*

beauty   music   rhythm
colour   nation   tradition
enjoy   noise

Discussion

What is the most enjoyable festival you have ever taken part in? Where/When/Why is it held?

What sort of preparations are necessary? When are they begun?

What happens on the day of the festival? Are any special clothes worn? Is any special food cooked?

Is anything arranged for the evening of the festival?

Do both adults and children take part in the festival? If so, are any special activities arranged for the children?

Is this festival still very popular nowadays?

Written tasks

1 Write a description of a popular festival which you have taken part in. Use the plan below as a guide.

Paragraph one

> **General introduction:** What is the name of the festival? Where/When/Why is it celebrated?

Paragraph two

> What preparations are made before the festival?

Paragraph three

> What happens on the day of the festival? Are any special meals cooked? What sort of ceremonies/celebrations take place?

Paragraph four

> **Conclusion.** Is there anything special arranged for the evening of the festival? How do people feel by the end of the day? Is the festival still popular these days? Why/Why not?

2 Write a description of a wedding or some other traditional ceremony in your country.

UNIT 14

Describing a book, play or film

This week, Susan is previewing forthcoming radio/TV programmes for the entertainments section of her paper.

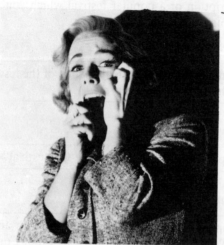

Tonight, the BBC continues its season of 'All-time greats'— a series which includes some of the most popular films of the past thirty years. Tonight's film is *Psycho*, a classic horror film directed by Alfred Hitchcock, and a masterpiece of its kind.

The film is set in America, and tells the story of a young man who runs a lonely, isolated motel with his elderly mother. They live in a large, old house next to the motel, but although we often hear their conversations, we never see the mother in person. A young woman stops at the motel one night, and in one of the most terrifying scenes of the film, is horribly and violently murdered. Her disappearance is soon noticed by friends, and they decide to find out what has happened to her. What follows is a spine-chilling tale of mystery and horror. Perhaps the most frightening part of the whole film comes in the last few minutes, when the identity of the murderer is revealed.

In spite of the fact that the film is now more than twenty years old, it is just as powerful as ever. Not only is it marvellously well acted, but it is superbly directed too, keeping the audience in suspense up to the very last moment. If you missed the film before, I strongly recommend that you see it tonight. A warning though — those of a nervous disposition might do well to have an early night instead!

Notes

A

Read the article and answer the following questions:

1 What information are we given in each of the paragraphs?
2 What is the function of the first and the final paragraphs?
3 Which tenses are used in the second paragraph to explain the plot of the film? Give examples.

B

Some examples of useful language are shown in the box on the right.

The film/story is set in . . .
It is a love story/a thriller/science-fiction . . .
It tells the story of . . .
It is about . . .
What follows is a . . . . . . tale of . . .
I greatly enjoyed . . . .
I was rather disappointed with . . .
It was well acted/directed/written.
It was rather long/confusing/unbelievable.
It is a classic/masterpiece of its kind.
I can/can't really recommend it.
It is well worth seeing/reading.

Word search

Find words in the text which correspond to the following:

a short period   very frightening
a film of the highest class   a terrifying story
is situated in   uncertainty/anxiety
motorists' hotel   suggest seeing it
section of a film   nervous by nature

Contrasting facts

> I was terrified *but* I enjoyed the film.
> *Although* I was terrified, I enjoyed the film.
> *In spite of the fact that* I was terrified, I enjoyed the film.

Join the following sentences in each of the ways shown above.

1 He loved her. He couldn't tell her.
2 He was badly injured. He managed to reach the frontier.
3 They were suspicious. They couldn't solve the mystery.
4 They were very poor. They were extremely happy.
5 I enjoyed the book very much. I didn't really like the film.

Inversion

> Not only was it well acted, but it was full of suspense, too.

Join the following sentences in the way shown above.

Example: He wins the race. He wins a fortune, too.
          *Not only **does he win** the race, but he wins a fortune, too.*

1 I have read the book. I have also seen the film.
2 The gangster shot a policeman. He also shot a passer-by.
3 She was late. She also forgot her notes.
4 She was still in danger. She was also getting very weak.

Relative pronouns

> The film tells the story of a young man *who* runs a motel.
> He owns a cat *that/which* never leaves the house.

Study the use of relative pronouns as shown in the examples above.
Then complete the text with the appropriate pronoun:

The film is about a secret agent _____ is sent to find out _____
is selling his country's secrets. He is given a number of secret
weapons, including a car _____ can go underwater and a watch
_____ shoots poisoned darts. Of course, eventually, he meets a
beautiful young woman _____ helps him to capture the spy and
_____ finally gives her life for him.

Vocabulary practice

Complete the sentences with an appropriate word from the list:

acting   chapters   filmed   scene
acts   ending   plot
audience   extremely   readers

1 The first three _____ of the book were very exciting.
2 The play consists of five _____ .
3 The film was _____ well directed.
4 The _____ clapped and cheered as the curtain came down.
5 Have you seen the film? What is the _____ ?
6 She won a prize for her marvellous _____ .
7 His death was the most moving _____ of the film.
8 _____ of science fiction will love this new novel.
9 Although I enjoyed the novel, I thought the _____ was rather disappointing.
10 The scene was _____ in Greece.

Discussion

Ask your partner about a play/book/film he/she has enjoyed recently. Find out:

— what type of film/book/play it is.
— why he/she chose it.
— where the story is set.
— who the main characters are.
— what the film/story is about. (What is the *plot?*)
— what he/she thought of it.
— if he/she would recommend it to the class.

Written tasks

1 Write a report on a film or play you have seen recently. Use the plan below as a guide and think about the tenses you will need to use in each paragraph *before you begin.*
Paragraph one

> **General introduction:** When did you see the film/play? Where? Who with? Why did you choose that particular film/play? What type of film/play is it?

Paragraph two

> Where is the film/play set? What is it about? Who are the main characters and what happens to them?

Paragraph three

> **Conclusion:** What was your opinion of the film/play? Why? Was it well acted/directed? Would you recommend it to others?

2 Write a report on an English book you have read recently. Collect the reports together and use them as a guide to the class library or as advice on further reading.

Writing guidelines, rules and regulations

Guidelines

Susan recently joined a local slimming club. She was given a diet sheet and also a set of guidelines containing some advice and suggestions for new members.

GUIDELINE FOR SLIMMERS

Welcome to our slimming club! Here are a few hints to help you succeed in your diet — please read them carefully and make them part of your daily routine.

EATING
Eat only the food listed on your diet sheet, and remember to weigh everything carefully before each meal. Make sure you start the day with a good, healthy breakfast, and be careful not to miss a meal, otherwise you may be tempted to eat snacks between meals.

DRINKS
You can drink as much tea and coffee as you like, but remember that a lot of soft drinks are fattening. Try a low-calorie drink instead.

RESTAURANTS
Wherever possible, avoid eating fried foods. If you know that will be difficult, try to eat less at other meals that day!

EXERCISE
This is a very important part of any diet. You should take at least 30 minutes' energetic exercise each day. Choose something you like — swimming, dancing, gardening — and get into the habit of doing some every day!

CHECKING YOUR WEIGHT
It is a good idea to weigh yourself at the same time of day each week. Remember to keep a weekly record of your weight so that you can see how much progress you are making.

Notes

A
Notice that written guidelines include items of both information and advice. Notice how each section is clearly headed *Drinks, Exercise* etc.

B
Some examples of useful language are shown in the box on the right.

C
Look again at the *Guideline for slimmers* and pick out examples of this advice language.

You should/You ought to . . .
It is a good idea to . . .
Don't forget to . . .
Remember to . . .
Make sure you . . .
Don't be afraid to . . .
Try to avoid -ing . . .
Don't . . . . . . or you will . . .
You shouldn't . . .
Be careful not to . . .

Word search

Find words or phrases in the text which correspond to the following:

sort of food to which someone is limited	be persuaded
	unit of energy supplied by food
regular way of doing things	a minimum of
piece of paper	a written account
to measure	
if not/or else	

Gerund or Infinitive?

Complete the following sentences. Supply the correct form of the verb.

1 Don't forget (bring) an umbrella with you.
2 Avoid (travel) by train, as services in this area are very poor.
3 It is a good idea (stay) with a family if you want to learn the language.
4 Remember (book) your hotel well in advance.
5 Be sure (leave) enough time to visit us before you go.

Giving advice

Climate
The weather here can be very changeable. Make sure you bring plenty of warm clothes and a good umbrella!

Some of your friends are coming to your country (or to Britain) for the first time. Write some information and advice which you might send to them before their visit. Think about:

— the weather.
— driving and transport.
— food/specialities of your region.
— restaurants and bars.
— entertainment.
— sporting facilities.
— places to visit.
— things to avoid.

Written task

Write a set of guidelines *either* for friends planning a foreign holiday in a country you have previously visited, *or* for friends planning a touring holiday in a popular tourist region of your country.

Rules and regulations

The notice below sets out rules and regulations for those using the countryside.

> **TAKE CARE OF THE COUNTRY! FOLLOW THE COUNTRY CODE**
>
> - Respect the countryside.
> - Keep your dogs under close control.
> - Guard against all risk of fire.
> - Do not leave gates unfastened.
> - Keep to public paths across farmland.
> - Help to keep all water clean.
> - Do not touch crops or machinery.
> - Protect wildlife, plants and trees.
> - Take special care on country roads.

Notes

Remember that notices must be quick and easy to read. For this reason the writer has used direct commands *Keep . . . Respect . . . Do not . . .*

Sometimes, however, direct Imperatives can sound impolite. In the hotel information sheet below, the writer has been careful to use *polite* commands and requests. Study the sheet and try to find some of these phrases.

```
                    HOTEL INFORMATION
                    ────────────────

BREAKFAST
Full English breakfast is available in the main dining hall
from 7am onwards. Please hang the card provided outside your
door before you go to bed if you would like continental
breakfast in your room.

OTHER MEALS
The main dining hall is located on the ground floor of the hotel.

                    Lunch  12 - 2
                    Dinner  7 - 10

Residents are requested not to smoke in the dining area.

SNACKS/DRINKS etc
Please call room service if you require refreshments.

PERSONAL BELONGINGS
The hotel accepts no responsibility for loss or damage.
Valuables may be deposited in the hotel safe.

FIRE PRECAUTIONS
You are advised to read the fire notice in your room on your
arrival and to check the position of your nearest fire exit.

DISCOTHEQUE
This is located on the ground floor of the hotel. Children
under 14 must be accompanied by an adult.

DEPARTURES
Residents are requested to vacate their rooms by 11am on the
day of departure.
```

Written tasks

1 Use the following prompts to write some rules and regulations for a large sports club.

1 Members/request/wear/jacket and tie/dining room.

2 You/advise/not leave/personal property unattended.

3 Please sign/book if/you want/bring in/guest.

4 Smoking/strictly forbidden/gymnasium.

5 You/request/phone/club/well in advance/if/want/cancel/booking.

> USEFUL LANGUAGE
>
> Please/Please do not . .
>
> You are requested to/not to . . .
>
> You are advised to/not to . . .
>
> . . . is strictly forbidden

2 Can you suggest any similar rules and regulations which you might find in the following places?

- at an airport
- at a public swimming pool
- at a zoo/safari park

3 You have been asked to help to write a formal information sheet which will be sent to new students coming to your school/college. You should include a brief description of the school/college and details of timetables, facilities and some of the rules and regulations. Set your information out under clear headings.

Writing a newspaper report

To start you thinking:

Do you ever read British newspapers? If you do, which ones do you read? (If possible, bring one to class.)

Do you like your newspapers to a) inform you about important events, b) entertain you, or c) do a mixture of both?

Do you think that the style of a newspaper which is mostly concerned with communicating important events will be different from that of a newspaper which is mostly trying to entertain? In what way will it be different?

The following article recently appeared in a local newspaper.

Notes

A

Notice that writing a newspaper report often requires the narrative techniques practised in Unit 9. The first paragraph may give a brief summary of the story, which is then expanded in the following paragraphs. The final paragraph often includes comments or quotations from a spokesman. What information are we given in each paragraph of this newspaper report?

B

A newspaper report often contains many Passive forms of the verb. Underline examples of these in this report.

C

How many different past tense forms can you find in the text?

TEENAGER ATTACKED ON WAY HOME FROM DISCO!

A 14-year-old boy was attacked and robbed on his way home from a disco last Saturday night. He was taken to a nearby hospital, but released soon afterwards with minor cuts and bruises.

Paul Janson spent the evening at a local disco, a short walk from his home. He left before his friends because he had promised not to be home late. As he was walking through Smith Park, a deserted and badly-lit area, he was attacked by a man he later described as dark-haired, of medium height and in his early twenties. The man took his wallet, containing £20, and his gold watch. Luckily, a car was just turning into Smith Street as the attack occurred. The driver saw what was happening, and rushed to Paul's assistance. The attacker then ran off in the direction of the High Street.

Police have warned local inhabitants to be on their guard and not to walk alone through the park after dark. 'Paul had a lucky escape,' a police spokesman commented, 'but the next victim might not be so fortunate'.

Narrative tenses

Which of the following sentences would it be correct to use when describing an attack which took place last week?

1 a) A boy has been attacked last Saturday night.
  b) A boy was attacked last Saturday night.

2 a) He spent the evening at a disco.
  b) He has spent the evening at a disco.

3 a) A car was just turning into Smith Street when the attack occurred.
  b) A car just turned into Smith Street when the attack occurred.

4 a) He left before his friends because he promised to be home early.
  b) He left before his friends because he had promised to be home early.

Word search

Find words in the text which correspond to the following:

allowed to go home

marks on skin caused by knocks or blows to the body

a dark area

happened

to his help

person speaking on behalf of a group

person who is the subject of an attack

Passives

ACTIVE	PASSIVE
A man attacked him.	He was attacked by a man.

Newspaper articles often contain examples of the Passive form of the verb, especially when they want to draw attention to the event itself, rather than the person responsible.

Change the following into the Passive form:

1 Someone mugged an old man yesterday.
2 They are questioning the attacker at the moment.
3 They will close the factory tomorrow.
4 They have signed a new peace treaty.
5 They had closed the road for six months.

Newspaper headlines

Writing a newspaper headline is similar to writing a message or a note. It is usual to omit articles, auxiliaries and some prepositions. Passive forms are also commonly used.

1 Say what the following headlines mean. Use complete sentences and be careful of tenses.

GOVERNMENT CRITICISED FOR NEW LAW

NURSE WINS £10,000

Woman mugged in Underground last night

POLICEMAN PRAISED FOR BRAVERY

FIRE IN LONDON HOTEL-TWO KILLED

2 Now suggest headlines for the following stories:

1 Someone rescued a man from drowning off a popular holiday beach yesterday.
2 The government has just introduced a new, tough law on drinking and driving.
3 Six people have been rescued from a sinking ship in the North Atlantic.

First and final paragraphs

Study the Notes on the first page of this unit and then write a first and a final paragraph for the newspaper report below. Before you begin think about the following questions:

Paragraph one
How many fans were injured?
Where was the match?
When was it?
Which teams were playing?

Paragraph three
Did a spokesman make any comment?
Were any lessons learnt for future matches?

VOCABULARY

surged forward
   moved forward in waves

a barrier
   something that controls movement

trapped
   unable to escape

trampled underfoot
   crushed under people's feet

a fleet of ambulances
   a number of ambulances working together

in a critical condition
   very seriously hurt

TWENTY INJURED AT FOOTBALL MATCH —

Paragraph one ....
....

Paragraph two

The accident happened when United scored their first goal. As fans surged forward, a barrier collapsed, and people were trapped and trampled underfoot. A fleet of ambulances took the injured to a local hospital, and twenty people have been detained. Two of these are in a critical condition.

Paragraph three ....
....

Written tasks

1 Thieves broke into a house in your neighbourhood a few days ago. Write the report which appeared in a local newspaper the next day. Use the plan below as a guide and the vocabulary in the box on the left to help you. Remember to use a suitable headline for your report.

Paragraph one

USEFUL VOCABULARY
to be horrified
to be insured
to damage
to force (a lock)
to overturn (furniture)
to slash (material)
to smash (a window)
to steal
fingerprints
insurance

Introduction: A short summary of events. Where did this happen? To whom? When? What was stolen?

Paragraph two

Development: Narrate the events as they happened. How did the thieves get in? Where were the usual occupants of the house? What did the thieves do? Was anyone hurt? Did anyone see the thieves?

Paragraph three

Conclusion: Have the police got any clues? Did anyone make a statement after the robbery?

2 Write a newspaper report about a special event (pop festival, sporting event etc) which took place in your area recently.

Giving opinions

To start you thinking:

Smokers

How many cigarettes do you smoke a day?
Do you worry about your health?
Have you ever tried to stop smoking?
Why do you think you smoke?

Non-smokers

How do you feel about people who smoke?
Do you think the price of cigarettes should be raised to stop people smoking?
Should smoking be banned in public places?
What exactly are these places?

Now find out what other members of the class feel about these questions.

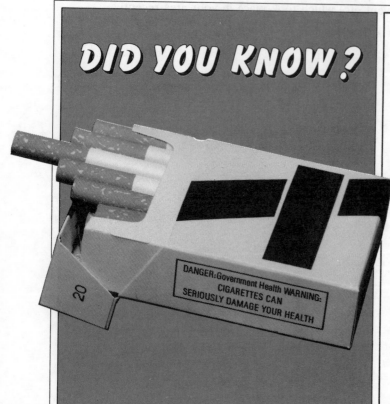

DID YOU KNOW?

It has been proved that the smoke from other people's cigarettes may affect your health.

In America, some companies have decided that if just one person protests, nobody else in that company is allowed to smoke at work.

In Glasgow, an organisation has been set up to make the whole city a no-smoking area by the year 2000.

DANGER: Government Health WARNING: CIGARETTES CAN SERIOUSLY DAMAGE YOUR HEALTH

Read the argumentative essay below. Do you agree with the writer's arguments? If not, say why not.

SHOULD SMOKING BE BANNED IN PUBLIC PLACES?

Statistics show beyond doubt that cigarette smoking can damage the health, yet a surprisingly large number of people continue to smoke in spite of all warnings. By doing so they are not just shortening their own lives, they are also affecting the health of those around them. It is time that non-smokers fought back!

Personally, I think smoking should definitely be banned in public places. In the first place, it is very unpleasant to sit in a smoke-filled room, such as a restaurant or cinema, if you do not yourself smoke. Added to this, smoking can be a serious fire risk, especially in crowded places like discos. Finally, in my opinion, nobody should be asked to risk his health just because of another person's bad habits.

Smokers may protest that they should be free to do as they like. They say that we already have no-smoking areas in public places, and that this should be enough. To my mind, however, non-smokers should also be free — free to go anywhere they choose without risking their health.

Smoking is harmful not just to smokers but to non-smokers too. If some people are foolish enough to continue this dangerous habit, it seems to me that they should at least be prevented from doing so in public.

Notes

A Look at the first sentence of each paragraph. Notice how the first sentence summarises the content of the paragraph. Which paragraph in the model does the following:

— gives the writer's opinion, and reasons for it?
— strongly restates the problem and the writer's opinion?
— sets out the problem in general and states why it is controversial?
— gives the other side of the argument and the reasons why this is false?

B Is the writer for or against smoking being banned in public places? How does the writer make his opinion clear?

Giving opinions

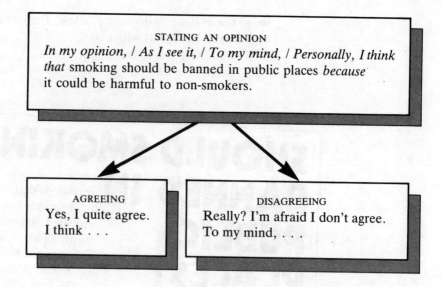

STATING AN OPINION

In my opinion, / As I see it, / To my mind, / Personally, I think that smoking should be banned in public places *because* it could be harmful to non-smokers.

AGREEING
Yes, I quite agree.
I think . . .

DISAGREEING
Really? I'm afraid I don't agree.
To my mind, . . .

1 Study the language shown above. We often use this when *speaking* about our opinions. Discuss the following topics in groups. Remember to give good reasons for your opinions.

1 Should the police carry guns?
2 Should car seat-belts be compulsory?
3 Should married women with children be discouraged from going out to work?
4 Should governments stop spending money on weapons and do more to help developing countries?

2 The language shown below can also be used when *writing* about our opinions.

In my opinion, / As I see it, / Personally, I think that . . .
because . . . I quite agree that . . . I don't agree that . . .

Write one sentence on each of the topics you have just discussed, stating your opinion and the reason for it.

Listing points

> Personally, I think that smoking should be banned in public places. *In the first place,* / *To begin with*, it is very unpleasant to sit in a smoke-filled room. *Added to this,* / *Furthermore,* / *Moreover*, smoking can be a fire risk. *Finally,* / *Lastly*, in my opinion nobody should have to risk his health just because of another person's bad habits.

1 The language in *italics* in the box above is used to list the points in an argument. In the same way, link the following points to make a complete paragraph.

Begin: *As I see it, married women with young children should* . . . .

SHOULD MARRIED WOMEN WITH YOUNG CHILDREN BE DISCOURAGED FROM GOING OUT TO WORK?

— Married women with children should be free to go out to work if that is what they wish.
— They should have the right to choose the sort of life they need to make them happy, without feeling trapped by marriage.
— Women can make just as important a contribution to the prosperity of their country as men do.
— There is no reason why companies can't provide nurseries where trained staff are employed to take care of young children during working hours.

2 Now use your own ideas to write a similar paragraph on *one* of the following questions:
Should the police carry guns?
Should governments stop spending money on weapons and do more to help developing countries?

Putting the other side

> Some people protest/argue that . . . They say/think that . . . To my mind, however . . .

In a discussion essay, it is a good idea to mention the other side of the case and then show why you do not agree. Think back to the topics you discussed on page 74. Did any members of the group disagree with your opinions? Why? Write a short paragraph on one of the topics discussed, setting out the arguments used against you, and then say why you think these arguments are mistaken. Use the language in the box above to help you.

Discussion

Discuss with a partner the following points about military service:

Is military service compulsory in your country for men and for women? How long does it last?

Have you done military service? What did you think of it? What sort of things did you learn? Were they useful?

Do you think women should do the same kind of military service as men? Why/Why not?

In what kind of situations do you think you might be called on to use the training? Do you think these situations are likely to happen?

Do you think the experience of doing military service makes someone a better or more disciplined person? Why/Why not?

Written tasks

1 Should military service be compulsory for all young men and women? Write a composition outlining your views, using the plan below to help you.

Paragraph one

> **General introduction**: What is the situation at the moment in your country/in the world? Is this a satisfactory situation?

Paragraph two

> Give your opinion and list the reasons for it.

Paragraph three

> Put the other side of the argument and then say why you disagree.

Paragraph four

> **Conclusion**: Summarise your arguments and restate your opinion clearly.

2 Is it better to be born a boy or a girl? Write a composition giving your views.

UNIT 18

Describing a place

To start you thinking:

Where did you spend your last holiday?
Why did you decide to go there?

Did you look at a travel brochure before you chose your holiday?
Did it give an accurate picture of your holiday choice? Why/Why not?

Were there any places of interest/historic towns nearby?
Why were they particularly famous?

What did you do in the evenings?

Now read the tourist brochure below about Stratford-upon-Avon.

Stratford-upon-Avon

Shakespeare's birthplace.

No visitor to Britain should go home without spending some time in Stratford-upon-Avon. Situated in the heart of England, it is a town rich both in history and in culture.

Stratford is a busy market town with a population of twenty-three thousand, and contains many streets and buildings unchanged since medieval times. It is surrounded by some of the prettiest countryside in England, and is an ideal base for those wishing to visit such places of interest as Warwick Castle, or the beautiful modern cathedral in Coventry.

Without doubt, Stratford is best known as the town where the playwright William Shakespeare (1564-1616) was born and died. Here you can visit his birthplace, and other buildings associated with his family. These houses are all splendid examples of Tudor architecture, and there are many other fine, historic buildings well worth visiting in the town.

Visitors to Stratford will find no lack of evening entertainment. There are restaurants to suit all tastes, and in the evening the Royal Shakespeare Theatre offers an exciting and varied repertoire, giving you the chance to see some of the best actors in the country, on stage. There are also poetry readings, music recitals and many other entertainments available.

Choose a holiday in Stratford and you will never forget the experience! Book now to avoid disappointment!

Notes

1 What is the writer of the brochure trying to do in his introduction and conclusion? Do you find the style persuasive? Why/why not?

2 Each paragraph deals with a different aspect of Stratford. What are these aspects?

Word search

Find words in the text which correspond to the following:

the centre of a town or country
period of history from about 11th–13th Century
a shortage of/not enough of
the author of a play
a programme of plays being performed at a theatre

Linking sentences

The town is situated in the heart of England. The town is rich in both history and culture.

↓

Situated in the heart of England, the town is rich in both history and culture.

1 Join the following sentences, beginning each new sentence with the Past Participle of the verb, as shown above.

1 The village is sheltered between high cliffs. The village is a popular holiday place.
2 The city is dominated by the cathedral. The city is an ancient, bustling place.
3 The town is hidden beyond a range of hills. The town has a busy, prosperous community.

2 Now write a similar sentence about your town/city.

Passives

Stratford *is surrounded* by some of the prettiest countryside in Britain.

1 Rewrite the following sentences using the more impersonal Passive construction:

1 People know the town best as a holiday resort.
2 They have recently built a new cathedral.
3 Someone discovered the island 200 years ago.
4 People say that ghosts inhabit the island. (People say that the island . . .)
5 People believe that a meteorite destroyed the forest. (People believe that the forest . . .)

2 Now write two similar sentences about your town. (Remember to use the Passive.)

The Gerund

> The town is an ideal base for (those) people who wish to visit the sights.

↓

> The town is an ideal base for *those wishing* to visit the sights.

Rewrite the following sentences using the Gerund, as shown above.

1 The town is an ideal resort for those people who want to spend their holiday skiing.
2 The city is an ideal place for those people who hope to do a bit of sightseeing during their trip.
3 The village is a perfect place for those people who plan to spend their time fishing and generally relaxing.

Vocabulary practice

Complete the sentences with an appropriate word from the list.

architecture	historic	resort	tourists
breathtaking	landscape	sightseeing	
guidebook	picturesque	sunbathe	

1 You will need to take a _____ so you don't get lost in the town!
2 The scenery was absolutely _____ !
3 Tourists _____ in London shouldn't miss a visit to Covent Garden.
4 They visited some _____ little villages.
5 Bournemouth is on the south coast of England and is a seaside _____ . Davos is a ski _____ in Switzerland.
6 Coventry Cathedral is a fine example of modern _____ .
7 It is dangerous to _____ at midday if you are not used to the heat.
8 In front of him, as far as his eye could see, stretched a snowy, mountainous _____ .
9 A _____ battle was fought just outside the town.
10 The villagers are suspicious of _____ .

Discussion

Use the following prompts to write questions and then interview your partner about his/her home town.

Which country/you/come from? Where exactly/your home/situated?
What/population?
What/town/like? What/surrounding countryside/like?
What/town/best known for?
Any historic buildings/places of interest/town?
Where/visitors/evenings? Theatres/shows?
Possible excursions/places nearby?
Your town/good place/holiday?

Written tasks

1 Write a description of a town/holiday resort in your country. It is to be included in a tourist brochure. Use the plan below as a guide. (You may change the number of paragraphs.)

Paragraph one

> **General introduction**: Why should visitors come to your town/resort? Where is it situated?

Paragraph two

> A general description of the town. Population? Surrounding attractions? Appearance?

Paragraph three

> Why is the town particularly worth visiting? Is it famous for its buildings/landscape/people?

Paragraph four

> What can visitors do in the evening? What sort of restaurants/clubs/entertainments can they find?

Paragraph five

> **Conclusion:** Write a few lines encouraging tourists to come to visit your town/resort.

2 Write a description of a town or city which you have visited recently.